Autumn Lovesong

Autumn Lovesong

A Celebration of
Love's Fulfillment
By Jesse Stuart

HALLMARK EDITIONS

Photographs:
Charles Steinhacker: Page 21, 24, 36, 44.
Toni Frissell: Page 25, 33.
P. Harrington © Look Magazine: Page 41.

To Naomi

Knee-deep in leaves, in milkweed furze
        with sawbrier trimming,
Your hand in mine to hold,
        your willowy body leaning
So your autumn-colored, curly hair is against
        my face and shoulder:
So deep in love, in autumn's splendor
        lucently dying,
So late in love our autumn is almost over,
Again we softly kiss, unmindful our time
        is inexorably going
To a secret place that is not
        beyond our knowing.

While time is left, let us pretend
        we are not caring
How little remains. We keep on living,
        loving, daring.

Come, put your shoulder
In the curve of my arm
Before we are older
And time is colder,
Turn on your charm.

Like under old leaves
Where lost youth repines,
Where late wind grieves
For love's old reprieves,
The late sun shines.

Higher and higher
Where the dim path goes,
By a late primrose,
There is more to admire
Where the late leaf goes.

Burnt-orange maple leaves
    drift indolently down,
Burgundy-wine chestnutoak leaves,
Buff-colored hickory leaves,
Tangerine-red sumac,
Apple-red persimmon,
Pumpkin-yellow sugartree,
Cockscomb-red maple
All rain their mixture to the ground.

We like the wind and leaf-rain sound.
Foxtail gray,
Ripe cornstalk brown,
Sumac-berry-red,
Turkey-wattles red,
Pumpkin-yellow,
Maroon,
Multicolored drops zigzag down
From the colored rainclouds
     to the ground.

Poplar leaves are the color
    of the bright full moon
On a winter night
    or an evening in June,
But the sere ash leaves
    are as grey-bellied
As a butterfly's winter-wan cocoon.

Come, my love, see a pair of terrapins
Trying to hibernate
Beneath these autumn winds,
Among these farewell-to-summers,
Terrapins in love are so considerate.

Watch them inching slowly down,
       embedding under
Earth's quilts of leaf and loam
For a long sleep
       in their temporary home
To be awakened in their cozy bed
By the next Spring's thunder.

This dirt becomes a mansion
Where these loves hibernate
In their traditional fashion,
To sleep, to dream and wait.

They will dream of the New Spring's love
     while they lie under
Until the southgone birds return
     to mate and sing;
Then, they will be awakened by Spring's
     heralding thunder,
Not by the songs of birds
     or warm, soft purring claws of rain.
Their resurrection will return to them
New love-life in an ambient,
     April spring.

Drowsy bumblebees, bumble,
    fumble, mumble
Over the hourly diminishing nectar left
    in each fairy cup
Of lavender-petaled, gold-centered
    farewell-to-summer blossoms.

The multicolored wings of hummingbirds,
    of bees and butterflies all tremble
When lean, impoverished yellowjackets
    fly in to break this happy love feast up
In this discerning, turning,
    burning season of last love
    that is autumn's.

Little black berries shine
    like a blacksnake's lidless eyes
Among the sweet wild honeysuckle vines
That summer-multiplied, climb upward
    to dwarf the struggling pines.
Their berries shine like lumps of coal
    around deserted mines.

And thorn-protected scottish thistles
>
men and women, agreeably, despise
Now send their gifts
>
of autumn's beautiful lovedeath,
>
most pleasing to all eyes,
Their muffy, fluffy furze-clouds,
>
upward to the windy skies.

An unidentified bird sings
      a weary lovesong for his mate,
Halfhidden in the maroon leaves
      on the wild sourvine.
This lonely bird is singing late.

We will not see
        nor hear again this autumn,
        where everything
Is lucently, beautifully,
        inexorably dying;
These winds will be pallbearers
        for each airlight corpse till spring,
Until new love is born tenderly,
        eagerly, like new infants' crying.
Balloons from milkweed pods
        now bursting in the sun
Are soft, white balls
        pitched by the southpaw wind.

Pick up a stick, my love, and bat!
　　Your umpire shouts, 'Strike one!'
The seconds tick. Lay down your stick.
You cannot hit curved balls
　　thrown by a southpaw wind
That come straight at you,
　　break and bend;
Like white rainbows in blue wind
　　they arch,
While we two lovers
　　on and on must march.

While there is time, we march
     and love and sing.

Do not swing again
     at the southpaw's sidearm pitch,
For the butterfly will need
     his pretty wing.

Come, my dear,
Let me hold your hand,
Something is near
In this beautiful land.

From springtime birth
We think and move

Upon this earth,
Direction: love.

We are winds crying
Over lost coves
While we are trying
To find the right loves.

Compatible,
Indefatigable,
Inescapable,
Unceaseable
Love.

There will not be time enough
        beyond the clock
To find what we are searching for:
Our old disloyalties recorded there
To harass, embarrass and to mock
When ancient winds moan for us
        in despair.

The higher we climb,
We get more sun.
First ledge is sweet thyme,
First victory is won.
In supreme elation,
Come, let us kiss.

Love's intoxication,
Love's adoration,
We must not miss.

With all living things
That sing and hum,
Through flaming trees
We have come.

The second ledge has views
        that are sublime,
Where drowsier, mumbling bumblebees
Put their last accents
        on the wasting flowers,
Where a mountain daisy blooms
        beneath the thyme,
Until plucked by this hand
        to fasten in your hair.

Pairs of barking squirrels play
     through the flaming trees
And pairs of birds, each to their kind,
     sing in the bowers,
Sing on their flights together
     through the air,
Sing everywhere!
On this high level there is no despair.

Unbored,
We have soared
On levels where life's patterns run,
Springtime with blossoms in our eyes,
With the bright wings of butterflies,
And summertime with growth and sun,
A time to shape and mould
     the things undone.
Unbored, we have soared,
Until older, yes, but none too wise,
For we have starlight in our eyes.

Unafraid,
We have made
Over half the circle of the clock
Ignoring its persistent tick-tock.

Enthusiastic, with time left to take
Love's elevator higher than the sun,
Since love is not measured by the sky,
But by the acts and deeds we have done.

Love is not measured by verse meter,
Nor by the wind,
Nor by the bees' last accents
    on the flowers.

True love cannot be bought and sold,
For it is all that it implies:
Substantial, and as certain
    as stars in the skies.

For many, true love
    is difficult to find
And, for a few, impossible to hold
    To engrave upon the heart and mind,
Since an ounce of it cannot be bought
With an acorn cup of fairy gold.

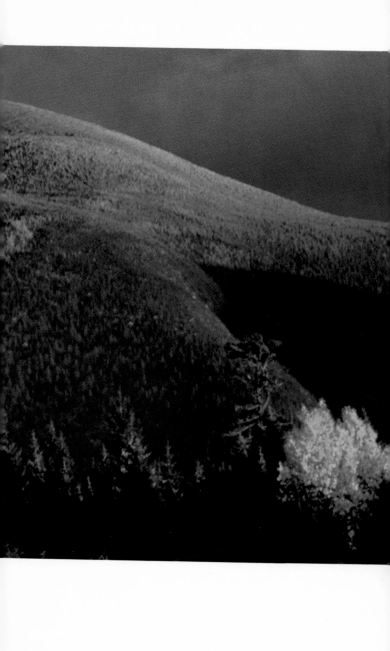

Up, up again,
Until the ridge plateau is won,
Our highest level under the sun;
And any way we look, on every side,
We see so high and far,
The moon, the sun and star

Will seem close by our side.

We know that love
    is high and deep and wide.

Up now, where love gone out of bounds
Will let us see
How high, how wide,
    how deep is this eternity.

It is no wider than our love is wide,
No deeper than our love is deep,
No taller than our love is true.
Love and eternity can go beyond the sky.
Love and eternity are not too much
For an acorn cup to hold
And the acorn cup can hold
A thimbleful of fairy gold.

Your lips, so like the color
    of the russet dogwood leaf,
In our love's journey
    we must not forget to kiss,
The season of the summer's blossoming
    is brief,
The season is uncertain for the petal
    and the leaf.

We must, we must, take time,
    take time, to kiss;
If we do not,
We miss.

Love is a hundred lives.

One life cannot compress
Emotions in the kingdom where love is,
A boundless universe, invisible within,
To mock and laugh and grieve,
Display its true emotions
        from the heart
And one, as fickle as the wind,
        upon the sleeve.
One never knows,
And one cannot guess
The way wind blows
Is happiness.

My arms entwine
Around your shoulder:
Your lips to mine,
Autumn is colder.

This is the time.

It is not too late.

Still green is thyme.

And lesser love
        cannot reach the sublime,
Can only hibernate.
Now, half around the clock
We hear and see,
Tick-tock, tick-tock.

True love will never come undone.

It is as big as all
Eternity
And higher than the sun.

Printed on Hallmark Eggshell Book paper.
Set in Romanee, a 20th century typeface designed
by Jan van Krimpen of Holland. Romanee was
created to accompany the only surviving italic of
the 17th century typefounder Christoffel Van Dijck.
Designed by Claudia Becker.